# THE SONG AT THE HEART OF THE RIVER

ishani naidu + kalyani ganapathy

First published in India in 2020 by HarperCollins Children's Books
An imprint of HarperCollins *Publishers*
A-75, Sector 57, Noida, Uttar Pradesh 201301, India
www.harpercollins.co.in

2 4 6 8 10 9 7 5 3 1

Text © Ishani Naidu 2020

Illustrations © Kalyani Ganapathy 2020

P-ISBN: 978-935-357-634-9

Ishani Naidu asserts the moral right
to be identified as the author of this work.

All rights reserved. No part of this publication may be reproduced, stored in a retrieval system, or transmitted, in any form or by any means, electronic, mechanical, photocopying, recording or otherwise, without the prior permission of the publishers.

Art direction by Kalyani Ganapathy

Printed and bound at
Replika Press Pvt. Ltd.

# A LETTER TO THE GROWNUPS

Many spiritual traditions see children as being closest to God. Their Souls have so freshly arrived to this world that they must be remembering the divine place from which they have come. Our desire for this book is to speak to the hearts of children and to the children within the hearts of adults. Though the wisdom of the Soul never leaves any of us, life and the mind have a way of becoming louder than the steady whisper of the all-knowing heart. Meaningful stories planted in us from childhood can be a guiding light from within, bringing us back to the Truth we knew at the moment we were born.

The spiritual science of Vedanta, developed by the Sages of Ancient India, contains a systematic roadmap back to understanding ourselves as we did as children. Free from the labels, expectations and confusions of adult life, we fully identify with our divine nature. The Sages of India also gave us Ayurveda, a comprehensive and holistic wellness system, to guide us in keeping our body, mind and senses balanced so that we are able to make the spiritual journey to reconnect with the origin of our Soul.

*The Song at the Heart of the River* is woven with core concepts from Ayurveda and Vedanta, with suggested activities for you and your child to play with the ideas yourselves. Though both of these knowledge systems originated thousands of years ago in India, you will happily discover their teachings are as globally applicable and potent today as ever.

With love and warmth,
Ishani

This book is an offering of deep gratitude to the teachers
who have brought this wisdom from a faraway time and
place and into our hearts and minds in this present moment.

With special appreciation for my Guru, Acharya Shunya,
whose powerful storytelling from her childhood experiences
of Ayurveda and Vedanta with her Guru prove the
transformative potential of stories.

From deep inside the Earth, where everything was perfectly still and quiet, a spring of fresh, clear water began to bubble up.

A tiny trickle wandered downhill across the soil and grew into a healthy, steady River.

The River's banks became home to many plants and animals.

Every morning, dawn's golden light sparkled across the River's surface, the ripples looking like thousands of small Suns.

An old man, lovingly called Baba, would come to the River every morning to feel the gentle glow of the rising Sun and sing about the strength and blessings of the Sun.

The River joined in, singing from deep within its heart, its own song blending together with Baba's joyful and steady voice.

Baba scooped up water in his palms and admired the Sun's reflection. As he poured the water back into the River, he delighted at the thousands of sparkling droplets that slid off his fingertips.

Where it was deep, the River would rest in quiet pools, softly swirling, before moving on.

Where it was shallow, it skipped and hopped, making cheerful music as it danced over the sandy shores and smooth pebbles.

Every day, children came to the River to splash and play.
Women brought clothes to wash while they talked and sang.

Tall reeds and delicate moss drank in the clear water and grew lush and green along the banks.

Seasons somersaulted, one into another. Fresh, juicy spring became hot summer.

Wet monsoon made way for a freezing winter, only to be melted by the glorious warmth of spring.

Then came a winter that was longer and darker than any other before. Clouds covered the sky and never left for what seemed like forever.

Fully enveloped in a thick blanket of fog, the Sun was totally blocked from sight. The River felt sleepier and sleepier. "Tomorrow the Sun will come wake me up and I will sing," the River drowsily told itself.

But the next day was as grey as the last, and slowly the River began to believe that the springtimes and songs of the past were just a dream — that there would never again come a day of light and warmth.

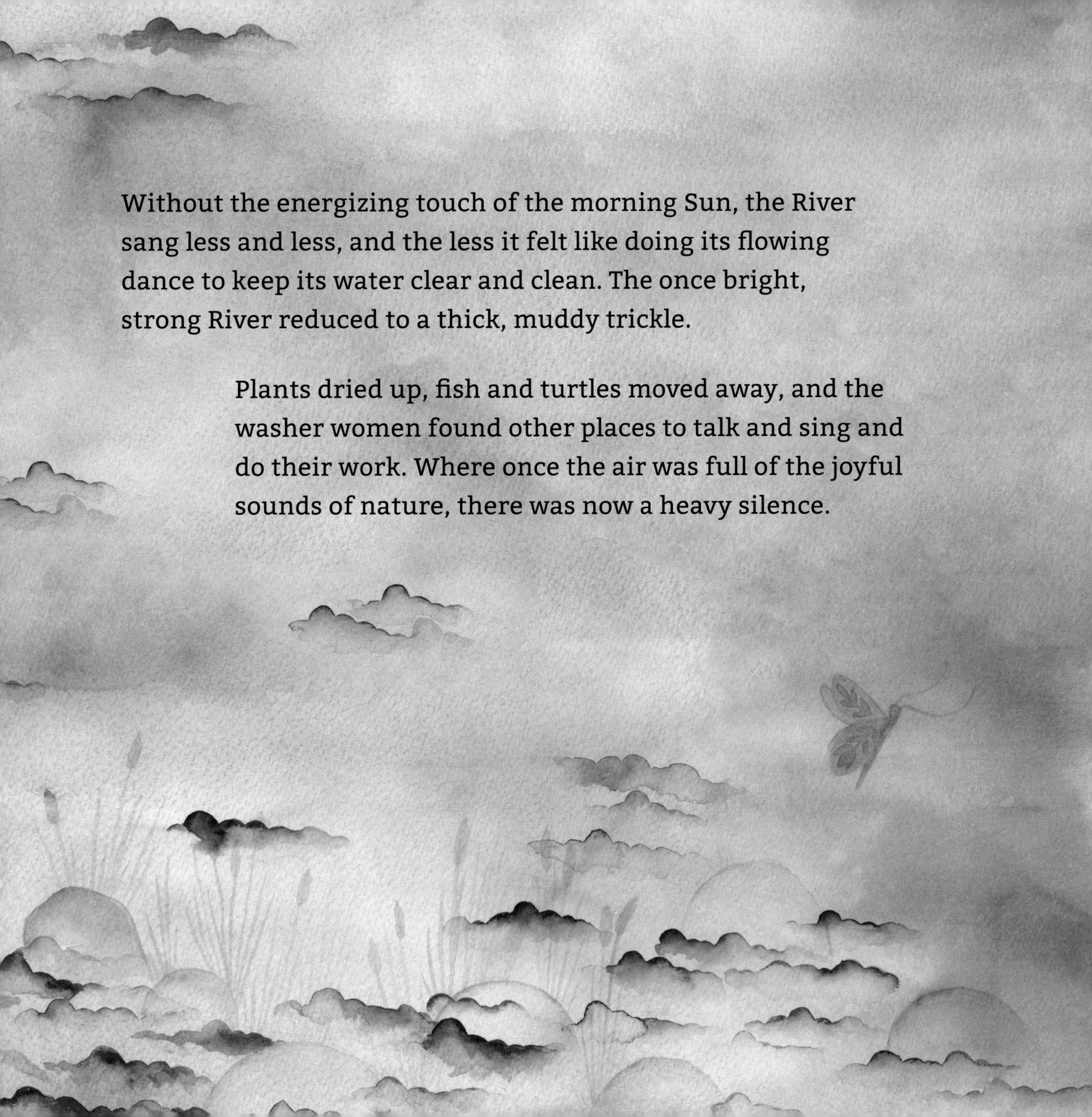

Without the energizing touch of the morning Sun, the River sang less and less, and the less it felt like doing its flowing dance to keep its water clear and clean. The once bright, strong River reduced to a thick, muddy trickle.

Plants dried up, fish and turtles moved away, and the washer women found other places to talk and sing and do their work. Where once the air was full of the joyful sounds of nature, there was now a heavy silence.

One day, while half asleep, the River heard something familiar. It was the sweet early morning song of Baba.

While the River had been missing the Sun, it hadn't noticed Baba still coming every morning as if nothing had changed. He was there holding a handful of sand from the dry riverbank and gazing at it as lovingly as he had when there was a sparkling Sun reflecting inside. Baba's song was as beautiful as ever.

This made the River's heart ache for the beauty and life that used to surround it. So many people, animals and plants had depended on the steady River and now it felt sorry for letting them down.

Even though it could hardly imagine that its own morning song was still hidden somewhere deep in its own heart, the River decided, "I have to find a way to do my river work again."

As if applauding that generous wish, a heavy cloud appeared above and dumped all of its rain in one crashing downpour!

With this encouragement, the River threw off its sleepiness and dove downstream. The bursting surge of water cleared the riverbed of mud and debris. Fun and play returned to the lifeless River.

Whooping and hollering, the River splashed and bounced along, finding new and different ways to make its way downstream.

Each moment was a noisy, exciting adventure. Free from all that heaviness, the River was eager to help its friends.

Hearing the River bubbling again, some children walking home from school made little paper boats. When they set them in the water, the over-excited River swallowed them up before the children could run downstream to catch them.

The washer women also came back with their laundry. The happy River made fast whirlpools to help scrub their clothes, but the current was so strong it pulled the clothes away and they were lost.

The River excitedly rushed fast and hard, picking up huge boulders along the way and dropping them in the riverbed.

The boulders made the River rough and created huge waves.

Mothers shook their fingers and warned their children, "Don't you go down to that river. It will drag you away downstream right along with it!"

Carried away in the excitement, without any time for rest, and unable to keep up the pace, the River's water reserves ran out. Without any more energy and missing its friends, it fell silent again.

Then the exhausted, lonely River caught the unmistakable sound of faithful Baba, singing to the rising Sun.

The long, dark winter had finally ended, but the River had been too busy rushing to even notice.

With time and rest, the River healed its friendships and built up its strength.

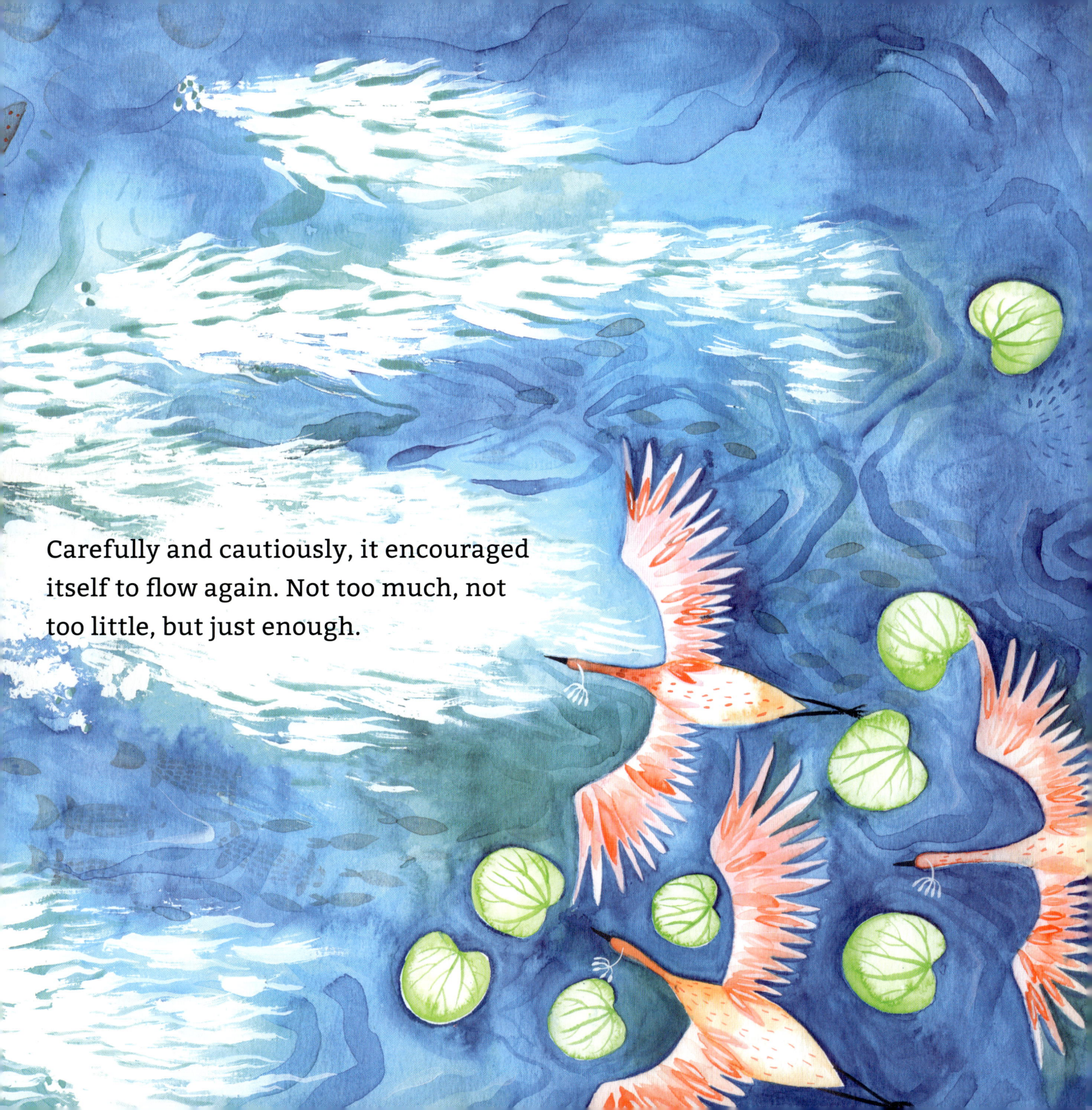

Carefully and cautiously, it encouraged itself to flow again. Not too much, not too little, but just enough.

Soon, the River started seeing the Sun everywhere — not only rising in the sky above and like thousands of mirrors shining on the water's surface, but also in the smiles of the children splashing.

It saw the Sun in the eyes of the women singing, in the nectar of the flowers, in the stones on the shore, in the feathers of the birds.

That same shining light seemed to be coming from everywhere. The River's heart filled with joy and its early morning song resounded more beautifully than ever.

# The Dynamic Qualities of Life

## SATTVA, RAJAS AND TAMAS

The Sages described three qualities or vibrations — called Sattva, Rajas and Tamas — that make up the entire universe. They are so subtle that we can't see them, but we can observe their actions in nature, in our bodies and in our minds. Everything from a grain of sand, to the planets in their orbit, to the thoughts we think are made up of different combinations of these three vibrations.

SATTVA is clarity, lightness, harmony, intelligence, and spirituality. Just like there can never be too much wisdom in this world, there can never be too much Sattva, as it serves to bring balance to the other two vibrations.

RAJAS is motion and activity. When it is healthy, Rajas helps us get out of bed in the morning, gets our bodies moving, changes our thoughts from one thing to another. When it is in excess, there is too much activity, volatile emotions, or exhaustion from not taking rest.

TAMAS is the quality of inertia and heaviness. It is the opposing force of Sattva and Rajas since it is dense and motionless. In moderation, we need Tamas to help us fall asleep at night, or to sit still during a class. When it is in excess, there will be laziness, negative thoughts, or feeling sorry for oneself.

Sattva, Rajas and Tamas are constantly dancing through our bodies, minds and nature. They bring the balance, change and stability needed for life. When we practice noticing how they change, we can understand the fluctuations in both ourselves and the world.

**THE RIVER'S JOURNEY HOLDS EXAMPLES OF SATTVA, RAJAS AND TAMAS IN VARIOUS STATES OF EXCESS AND BALANCE.**

Have fun searching for the picture clues on this page, by flipping the pages and finding them.

When you spot one, pause and consider what is happening to the River at that time — what it is doing, how it is feeling. Which of the qualities is dominant in the story where the image appears? Talk to each other about how that can be an example to further understand the three dynamic qualities of life.

1)

2)

1) Sattva 2) Healthy Tamas 3) Healthy Tamas 4) Sattva 5) Tamas in excess 6) Tamas in excess 7) Rajas in excess 8) Sattva 9) Healthy Rajas 10) Healthy Rajas 11) Rajas in excess

# MODERATION

## AN AYURVEDIC KEY TO HEALTH

Too much or too little of anything is not good. Ayurveda tells us that just the right amount of everything will keep our whole health balanced. In the following activity, we playfully imagine extremes, and moderation reveals itself as something to look forward to.

First, imagine what Not Enough, Too Much and Just Right would look like in these examples...

### EATING CAKE AT YOUR BIRTHDAY PARTY

*Not Enough:* you won't enjoy your celebration treat.

*Too Much:* you will have a tummy ache. Ouch!

*Just Right:* you get to enjoy the cake and feel good to play at your party all day.

## SHAMPOOING YOUR HAIR

*Not Enough:* your hair won't get clean and will be a tangled mess.

*Too Much:* you will be covered in bubbles and the shampoo will go in your eyes.

*Just Right:* hair gets clean without shampoo going all over the rest of your face.

Now give these a go:

1) PLAYING OUTSIDE 2) TALKING TO YOUR FRIENDS WHEN THEY COME OVER TO PLAY 3) PLAYING GAMES ON THE COMPUTER 4) ADDING LAYERS OF CLOTHES TO WEAR IN THE SUMMER 5) LISTENING TO MUSIC 6) DRINKING WATER 7) BLOWING YOUR NOSE 8) WATERING A PLANT

Now make up your own scenes.

# THE SUN

## AND ITS RELATIONSHIP TO THE INDEPENDENT SELF WITHIN

In Vedic tradition, the Sun is seen as a powerful symbol of pure consciousness. Many hymns and mantras from Ancient India sing the virtues embodied by the Sun, and we are told that contemplating on those qualities will increase our physical, mental, social and emotional wellbeing.

The practice called *Sandhya Vandanam*, which you see Baba doing in this story, is still a widely practiced ritual of worshipping the Sun at certain times of the day. As with all Vedic methods of worship, it seems like we are honouring some object outside, but we are really worshipping the divine qualities it represents that exist within ourselves.

## Qualities of the Sun we can connect with inside ourselves:

### RELIABILITY
the Sun rises every day no matter what.

### STEADINESS
the Sun always travels on a predictable path through the sky, at a predictable time.

### POWER
the Sun's radiance is the charge that powers the growth and life of all plants, animals and human beings.

### GENEROSITY
the Sun is selflessly giving its light energy to all beings everywhere, without asking for anything in return, regardless of what they look like, act like, what they believe, etc.

### INDEPENDENCE
all the light of the Sun comes from within, it does not depend on anyone or anything to make it powerful or give it approval or tell it how much to shine. While many others depend on the Sun, the Sun depends on no one.

# A HEALING FAMILY RITUAL

**EVERY MORNING, WHEN YOUR CHILD WAKES UP, TAKE THEM OUTSIDE OR TO A WINDOW FACING THE RISING SUN IN THE EAST.**

Create a personal ritual for the two of you to share: sing a quiet song welcoming the day, talk about how the glowing sun is giving both of you its energy and blessings for the day, simply cuddle and enjoy this special moment of stillness before the day begins, water a special plant together, imagine a Sun just like the one you are seeing glowing in your hearts.

## What does this practice do for you and your child?

- Eases you into the morning routine with a calm and natural awakening for less struggles getting ready in the morning.

- Synchronizes your bio-rhythms with the Sun cycle for countless mental and physical health benefits.

- Cultivates a special connection between you and your child.

ISHANI NAIDU is a native of the California Bay Area, USA and currently lives with her husband and two young children in Coimbatore, India. She conducts talks and workshops for children, teens and adults on awakening body and mind health awareness and creating a lifestyle that promotes holistic wellbeing with Ayurveda and Vedanta. Her writing can be found at *www.wholepeace.in.*

She continues to study closely with her teacher of over a decade, Acharya Shunya. Visit *www.acharyashunya.com* for more authentic, oral tradition teachings of Ayurveda, Yoga and Vedanta.

KALYANI GANAPATHY lives in the Nilgiris, India where she grew up. She is a self-taught illustrator and art director. Kalyani illustrates both fiction and non-fiction.

She loves bringing children's books to life. Her work has been featured in books and publications in India and abroad. Her children's books include *Hambreelmai's Loom, A is for Anaar, Janice Goes to Chinatown* and *Amrita Sher-Gil, Rebel with a Paintbrush.* Visit *www.kalyani-ganapathy.com* for more.